THE BASICS OF
SOUND

THE BASICS OF SOUND

CHRISTOPHER COOPER

This edition published in 2015 by:

The Rosen Publishing Group, Inc.
29 East 21st Street
New York, NY 10010

Additional end matter copyright © 2015 by The Rosen Publishing Group, Inc.

Library of Congress Cataloging-in-Publication Data

Cooper, Christopher.
The basics of sound/by Christopher Cooper.
        p. cm.—(Core concepts)
Includes bibliographic references and index.
ISBN 978-1-4777-7766-4 (library binding)
1. Sound—Juvenile literature. I. Cooper, Christopher (Christopher E.). II. Title.
QC225.5 C66 2015
534—d23

Manufactured in the United States of America

© 2004 Brown Bear Books Ltd.

CONTENTS

CHAPTER ONE

SOUNDS IN THE AIR

The air that surrounds us gives us more than life—it also gives us the rich world of sound. The air carries sounds to our ears, and our nerves and brains convert those sounds into the experience of music, voices, and the activity of the world around us.

Sound is a disturbance of the air. We are able to hear things because there is air between us and the things that cause the sound. Sound is a particular kind of disturbance: it is a vibration. Not all disturbances of the air, however, are vibrations. The wind consists of a movement of the air from one place to another, revealed by the movement of clouds across the sky or by scraps of paper blown along a street. But the movement of air that carries a sound is not so obvious because it does not make the air move as a whole. Instead, the tiny particles, known as molecules, that the air is composed of vibrate individually—at each place they move backward and then forward without any overall change in their position (unless there is a wind blowing).

GOOD VIBRATIONS

Although we cannot see air, we can get an impression of what the vibrations

SOUNDS IN THE AIR | 7

of molecules in air are like by comparing them with the movement of water. Water moves from place to place in rivers and streams, in ocean currents, and in the flow from a faucet. These water movements are like the movement of air in winds. But waves in water are different. There can be waves even in calm water—on a lake, for example. These waves move along, but the water does not move along as a whole. A boat floating on the lake is not carried along; instead, it bobs up and down. As a wave passes beneath the boat, the individual molecules of water make a circular movement, going backward and forward and up and down. When the wave has passed, the molecules will have scarcely changed their positions, and neither will the boat. Sounds are waves in the air. A sound wave in still air travels on, while individual molecules in the air merely vibrate around a particular position.

Sometimes we become aware that sound consists of vibrations. Very deep sounds consist of very slow vibrations of

A fusillade of fireworks makes a riot of sound. Each small explosion sends a shock wave through the air that creates the sensation of sound in listeners when it strikes their eardrums. When sound consists of carefully selected and controlled tones, we find it pleasant and call it music. When sound is disorderly and uncontrolled, we call it noise. Some noises, such as the sound of a brook, or rustling leaves, can be pleasing. Others can be unpleasant; and others, like the sounds of fireworks, startling or thrilling.

the air (for the relationship between the rate of vibration and the pitch of a sound, see pages 10–11). A very deep, very loud note on a church organ can be felt as a throbbing that affects the whole building.

ZONES OF COMPRESSION

In a sound wave the molecules of air get more or less crowded together. You can see a similar sort of wave in a long, flexible spring, such as the toy springs that "walk" downstairs by themselves. Imagine the

COMPRESSION WAVES

When sound radiates outward from a source, air does not move away from the source as a whole. Instead, the particles in the air, called molecules, vibrate backward and forward. Where the molecules are squeezed closer together, they are said to be compressed. Where they move apart, they are described as rarefied. The movement of the sound wave is the movement of this pattern of crowding and spreading out. It is like the "wave" in a football stadium: People do not leave their seats, but stand and sit in succession so that a wave of motion goes through the crowd.

Compressed   Rarefied

Area of compression moves forward

spring is hanging from one end. Jiggling the bottom end of the spring squeezes the coils of the wire closer together, with each coil pushing the next above it, and waves of compression move up the spring, separated by zones where the coils are momentarily stretched.

Air acts as if it were a spring. When something vibrating, such as the skin of a drum, briefly "jiggles" it, waves of compression travel outward. In these zones of compression molecules in the air are crowded together. Between adjacent zones of compression the molecules are more thinly spread—the air is "rarefied." As the waves pass by, the molecules do not change their position—they vibrate backward and forward, first in the direction the wave is moving, and then in the opposite direction.

TIMBRE, PITCH, AND NOISE

How we perceive a sound depends on our ears and brains. We cannot hear vibrations of the air that are very slow or very fast (see chapters seven and eight). We cannot hear vibrations in which the molecules make only very small movements; and vibrations that are very large hurt our ears and can even damage our sense of hearing, perhaps permanently (see pages 44–45).

Sounds vary not only in their loudness and pitch but also in their distinctive quality, or "color," which is called "timbre" (pronounced tam-ber). Notes played on a piano, a violin, and a flute sound quite different even when they all have the same pitch; the distinctive quality that enables us to recognize the instrument is the timbre. These differences all result from the different and complicated vibrations of the air molecules. Sounds from most instruments have a definite pitch—each note produced is distinct and different. A mixture of sounds with no definite pitch, as from an explosion, is called noise.

This explosion is an uncontrolled release of energy that creates a devastating blast wave in the air. The blast consists of air rushing outward and travels only a short way. But beyond the blast sound waves are created that consist of air vibrating backward and forward. These waves travel long distances.

CHAPTER TWO

SOUND BEHAVIOR

Sound can be surprisingly loud in some situations and faint in others. It can go around corners, and it can make echoes. The behavior of sound can be understood by thinking of it as a wave motion. Sound waves, like other waves, have certain important features, including their wavelength and frequency, and the speed at which they travel.

To understand the behavior of sound waves, it is necessary to know something about waves in general. Water waves give the clearest illustration. The distance from one peak of a wave to the next (or from one trough to the next) is called the wavelength.

In sound waves, corresponding to the peaks and troughs of water waves are places where the air molecules have shifted the most from their initial positions in the forward direction, and others where they have shifted the most in the backward direction. The distance from any one "peak" to the next one, or from any one "trough" to the next one, is the wavelength of the sound wave.

Sound travels faster through solids, such as these steel railroad tracks, than it does through air.

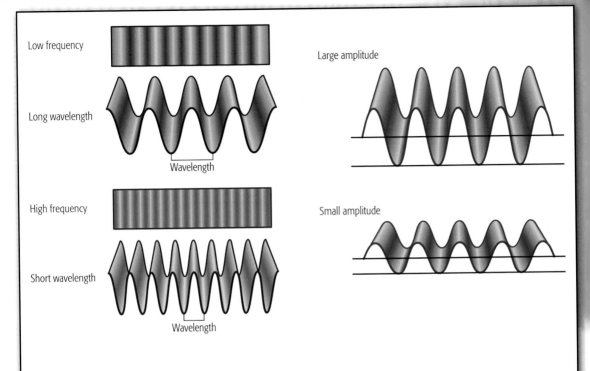

Low frequency

Long wavelength

Wavelength

High frequency

Short wavelength

Wavelength

Large amplitude

Small amplitude

FREQUENCY, WAVELENGTH, AND AMPLITUDE

For any wave the wavelength is the distance from one peak (or trough) to the next. The shorter the wavelength, the more waves pass a fixed point each second—that is, the higher the frequency. Amplitude is related to the intensity, or strength, of a wave.

The number of waves passing a given point every second is called the frequency of the wave. The frequency of the wave multiplied by its wavelength is the speed of the wave (speed = number of waves passing per second × the length of each wave). Under the same conditions all sound waves move at approximately the same speed. This means that higher-frequency waves have shorter wavelengths, and lower-frequency waves have longer wavelengths.

Waves in water can be large or small. The height of a wave above the level of calm water is called its amplitude. The amplitude of a sound wave is the distance the air molecules move from their rest positions. The more violent the disturbance that causes the sound, the greater the amplitude and the louder the sound.

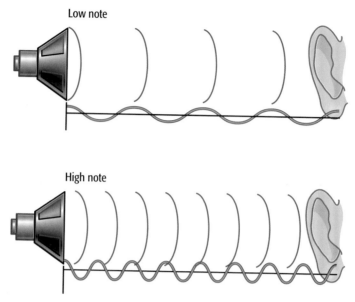

CHANGE OF PITCH

In a sound wave the shorter the wavelength, the higher the pitch. Pitch can change without any change in the amplitude, or loudness, of the sound.

Waves in the ocean move water molecules much the same way that sound waves move molecules of air.

The special shape of a whispering gallery, such as the one in St. Paul's Cathedral, in London, allows sound waves to travel in such a way that whispers in one area can be heard clearly in other areas.

SUBSTANCES AND SPEEDS

Sound must have something to travel in, and it travels faster in some substances than in others. The speed of sound in air, for example, is about 330 meters per second (about 1,080 feet per second). As a result, it takes approximately 3 seconds for sound to travel 1 kilometer (or 5 seconds to travel 1 mile).

Sound travels faster in liquids than it does in air and other gases. In pure water its speed is about 1,500 m/s (about 4,900 ft/s) and slightly higher in seawater. Sound travels fastest of all in solids. Its speed is about 5,000 m/s (16,500 ft/s) in steel, and in a hard rock such as granite it is about 6,000 m/s (19,700 ft/s). The sound of an approaching train, for example, can be heard as vibrations of the railroad lines before the sound of the locomotive reaches our ears through the air. That is because sound travels 15 times faster in steel than it does in air.

CHAPTER THREE

STRINGED INSTRUMENTS

Stringed instruments date from before the beginning of recorded history. Taut strings can be plucked, struck, or rubbed with bows to create sounds as different as those of the harp and the violin. They can produce this variety of sound because it is possible for many waves to vibrate along the length of a single string at the same time.

Many types of musical instrument have taut strings that vibrate when they are struck or plucked or rubbed. Each stretched string vibrates with a certain frequency that is natural to it. This in turn sets the air in motion, making it vibrate at the same frequency as the string does. The vibration dies away if the string is plucked or struck once. But if the string is scraped with a bow (which is a set of taut horsehair strings stretched by a flexible wooden rod), the continued force keeps the string vibrating. The string makes a sustained note, but the note is still of the same frequency.

In any note produced in this way there are actually other, higher, frequencies mixed in with the main frequency, which is known as the fundamental. However, to understand how

The instruments in the string section of an orchestra cover the different pitch ranges from the double bass, which is the deepest, through the cello and viola, to the violin.

musicians produce different notes on stringed instruments, it is easier if we start by imagining that the fundamental is the only frequency present.

TENSION, PITCH, AND LENGTH

The frequency of vibration of a string depends on its tension. If you pull the string more tautly, the pitch goes up. It falls again as you slacken the string. When a guitarist tunes up, you can hear the notes from the strings rising and falling. Rock guitarists make use of this effect in their playing when they use the tremolo arm. It "wobbles" the bridge, the device on the body of the guitar to which the strings are attached. That alters the tension of the strings slightly, making the pitches of the notes being played "wobble" too.

When the tension in a string does not vary, the pitch of the note it gives out depends on its length. The shorter the string is made, the higher the note it produces. A harp has its characteristic shape because it is simply a set of strings, each with its own fixed length and providing a note in the range that is covered by the instrument. Players of bowed instruments vary the length of the strings by pressing the strings against the neck of the instrument, known as "stopping" them, at varying positions. Guitarists do the same, but there are ridges or bars called frets set into the neck of the guitar, providing a fixed endpoint for the string.

One of the earliest discoveries of mathematical patterns in nature was made by the Greek philosopher Pythagoras, or one of his followers, in the 6th century B.C. He found that the notes produced by a string depend in a simple way on its length. If the length of the string is halved, the string produces a new, higher note that is harmonious with the original note. In fact, it is one octave above the original note. (The sequence of eight notes in the major scale, do, re, me, fa, so, la, te, do, cover one octave.) Harmonious

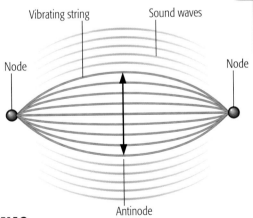

VIBRATING STRING

The simplest way in which a string can vibrate is when there are just two stationary points, called nodes, one at each of its ends, and the maximum movement is at the center, called the antinode. The vibration of the string sets up vibrations of the air, or sound waves, with the same frequency.

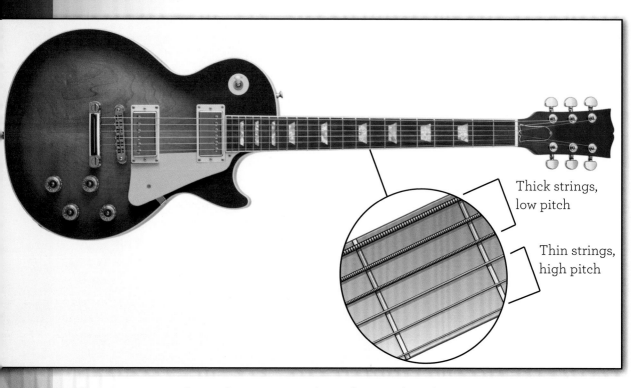

Thick strings, low pitch

Thin strings, high pitch

The note given out by a vibrating string depends on its length, tension, and weight per unit length. The six strings of an electric guitar are all metal. The three with the highest pitch are single wires, the thinnest and lightest giving the highest pitch. The three lowest strings are made heavier by winding a second metal wire around a thicker steel wire core.

notes are also produced when the string is stopped at two-thirds and four-fifths of its original length. The discovery that these simple ratios appeared in an apparently complex field like music was one of several scientific findings that persuaded Pythagoras and his followers that the entire world is somehow built around numbers and simple fractions.

Another very important feature of the strings in musical instruments is their weight. If two strings of the same length are stretched equally tightly, the one that is heavier will vibrate more slowly and give out a note of lower pitch. That is why the low-pitched strings of instruments are noticeably thicker and heavier than the higher-pitched strings.

HARMONICS

The note from a vibrating string is not "pure"—if you listen carefully, you can hear different notes present in it. And slowing down a close-up motion picture of the string shows that at each moment it forms a "wiggly" line that is not a simple wave shape.

The complicated shape of the string at each moment is built up from simple wave shapes. In the illustration below, waves with three wavelengths are shown. The shortest wave has one-third the wavelength of the longest and three times the frequency; the middle wave has one-half the wavelength and twice the frequency. The string is shown vibrating in each of these ways in turn. It can be made to do this by stopping the string at one of the stationary points shown, which are called nodes. But if the string is not interfered with, it will vibrate in all these ways at the same time. Most of its movement will be like the fundamental, but a small amount of the first harmonic will be mixed in, and a still smaller amount of the second harmonic. There will also be smaller and smaller amounts of still higher harmonics, making a very complicated waveform. It is this that gives the timbre to the note of the string, making it sound very different from, say, a trumpet playing a note of the same fundamental pitch.

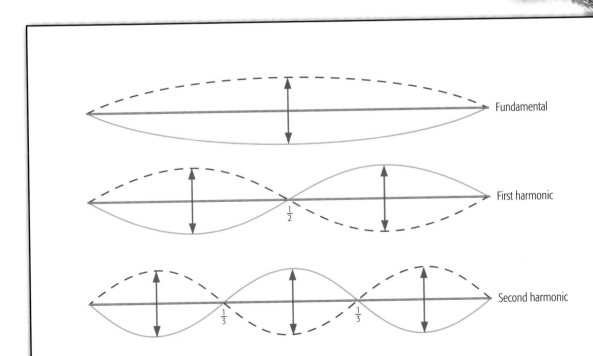

FUNDAMENTAL AND HARMONICS

When a string vibrates at its fundamental frequency, half a wavelength fits into the string's length. The first harmonic is a vibration with a wavelength equal to the length of the string and a node halfway along the string. The second harmonic has a wavelength equal to two-thirds the length of the string, with nodes one-third of the way from each end.

CHAPTER FOUR

THE MUSIC OF MOVING AIR

Organs, trumpets, flutes, and the human voice have something in common: They make sound because a volume of air is vibrating inside them, not something solid. The job of the player—or speaker— is to control the amount of air that vibrates at each moment.

Most of the sounds that we hear have been caused by something solid vibrating and setting up vibrations in the air. But it is also possible for a quantity of air trapped inside some kind of enclosure to vibrate, causing vibrations in the air outside the enclosure that spread out freely as sound waves. An easy way to make

In a pipe organ each note is played by a separate pipe. Air is blown into the mouth of the pipe to sound the note.

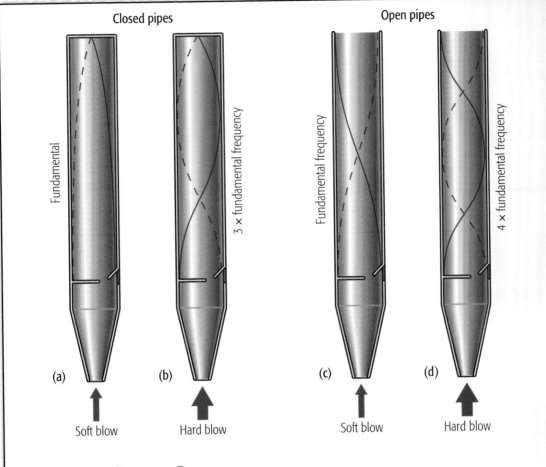

Closed pipes
Open pipes

(a) (b) (c) (d)

Soft blow   Hard blow   Soft blow   Hard blow

Fundamental

3 × fundamental frequency

Fundamental frequency

4 × fundamental frequency

OPEN AND CLOSED PIPES

The closed end of a pipe is a node (zero-vibration point) of the sound waves. Open ends are antinodes (maximum-vibration points). Blowing fairly softly sounds the fundamental, as in pipes (a) and (c). More and more harmonics can be set up as the pipe is blown harder, as in pipes (b) and (d).

this happen is to blow across the mouth of a bottle. When you blow at the correct angle, you will produce a loud, musical note that is made by the air inside the bottle vibrating.

You can "tune" the bottle to make notes of a different pitch by pouring in some water. The new note will be higher than the first one because the amount of air inside is less. You can set up a number of bottles tuned to different notes in this way and play tunes on them.

The same principle is used in wind instruments. The air in the pipe or tube

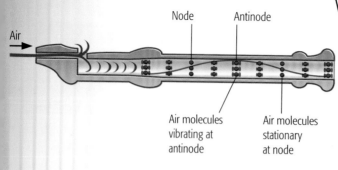

Node   Antinode

Air →

Air molecules vibrating at antinode

Air molecules stationary at node

WOODWIND INSTRUMENTS

In the recorder and penny whistle, two members of the flute family, the player closes holes with the fingers while blowing into the mouthpiece. Waves are set up with nodes at the closed holes, and this determines the pitch of the note that is produced (here all the holes are closed).

of the instrument vibrates to make the sound. The longer the column of air that vibrates, the deeper the note.

Organs are instruments consisting of a set of pipes, each playing a single note. Air is blown into the pipes mechanically. Originally an assistant had to keep working bellows to blow air into an airtight box while the organist was playing. This kept a high pressure in the box that continually forced air into the pipes. Nowadays the air pressure in the box is kept high by an electric fan. The organist uses hands and feet to press keys that allow air into whichever pipes are needed at each moment.

Bagpipes consist of a bag into which the piper blows air to keep up a constant pressure. The bag forces air steadily through the pipes. Pipes called drones produce steady low notes. A higher-pitched pipe called a chanter has holes that the piper closes.

Brass players make their lips vibrate as they blow, which makes the air in the instrument vibrate. They alter the length of the vibrating column of air by moving keys that alter the effective length of the airway in the instrument.

In some organ pipes, called flue pipes, the air passes in through a specially shaped inlet that sets up the vibration. In others, called reed pipes, the air passes over a piece of flexible metal called a reed, and it is this that vibrates, setting the air in the pipe vibrating. Similar sorts of air inlet appear in other types of wind instrument.

One of the simplest of all wind instruments is the penny whistle. It is basically a tube with a shaped mouthpiece, called a fipple. The tube is open at the other end, too. There is a series of holes along the pipe. By closing the holes with his or her fingers, the player alters the effective length of the pipe and thus the pitch of the sound.

PITCH AND WAVELENGTH

The pitch or frequency of the sound made by a vibrating column of air depends on its wavelength. The wavelength of a vibration is related to the distance from one node (a place where there is no vibration) to the next, or from one antinode (a place where there is maximum vibration) to the next. Opening and closing holes in a musical instrument alters the positions of antinodes, thus affecting the wavelength of the vibrations and the frequency of the sound.

The open end of the pipe is the position of one antinode because the air there is completely free to vibrate. The mouthpiece marks another antinode.

The longest wave that can be set up in the pipe has antinodes at the two ends and one node between them. The length of the pipe is half a wavelength—the distance from one "peak" of the wave to the next "trough" (as in pipe (c) in the illustration on page 19).

Some organ pipes are closed at one end. There is always a node of the vibration at this end. The longest wave that can be set up in such a pipe is the one that has no other nodes within the pipe. The length of the pipe contains one-fourth of a wavelength (as in pipe (a) in the illustration on page 19).

This longest possible wave is the fundamental of the pipe. It is the note that predominates in the sound, though

harmonics can be set up in addition if the player blows hard.

If the player opens a hole, say, two-thirds of the way down the pipe, a new wave will be formed with an antinode at this position because the air in the pipe can then vibrate freely, with the vibration escaping into the air outside the pipe. The new fundamental note will have a wavelength two-thirds that of the previous fundamental, and a frequency that is one and a half times as great.

WIND INSTRUMENTS

Both the recorder and the flute are fundamentally the same kind of instrument as the penny whistle. Clarinets and

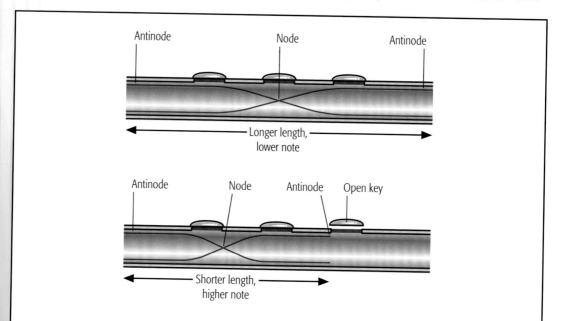

THE CONCERT FLUTE

In the concert flute each hole is closed until the player presses a key that uncovers it. Uncovering a hole effectively shortens the pipe. An antinode forms here, and shorter waves, with higher pitch, are set up.

Early flutes were often made from the bones of animals. Flutes as old as 35,000–40,000 years old have been found, making the flute one of the earliest known human instruments.

saxophones differ in having a reed to provide the vibration; oboes and bassoons have a pair of reeds that vibrate against each other. All of these instruments are known as woodwind because originally they were made of wood, though today many flutes (and all saxophones) are made of metal. The holes along their length remain closed unless the player presses keys to open them and change the pitch of the note.

Another family of wind instruments consists of the brass instruments. In them the vibration is made by the player's lips. The variations in the length of the vibrating air column are achieved by channeling the air through different lengths of pipe. In the trumpet, French horn, tuba, and other instruments the length is varied by pressing keys. In the slide trombone it is done by moving the slide in and out to vary the length of the pipe continuously.

CHAPTER FIVE

VIBRATIONS AND SOLIDS

The first primitive music apart from song must have been the bangs and crashes made by knocking objects together. Over the thousands of years since then percussion instruments have been developed into sophisticated devices. Percussion is more important than ever before in serious music and often dominates rock and pop.

When you tap two pebbles together, you are unlikely to hear anything that is more interesting than a dull click. Hollow objects generally make louder and more musical notes than solid ones. This fact is used by detectives and customs officials when they tap the bottom of a suitcase to see whether there is a hollow inside it in which something could be hidden and smuggled into the country.

A hollow log can make a booming noise. Dried seedcases or gourds (a type of large, hollow fruit) make sharp,

Drum sets consist of several types of drums and cymbals. Their sounds fall into different ranges, and they can have different qualities or "colors" of sound according to the way in which they are struck.

The xylophone consists of wooden bars, or keys, whose pitches are carefully set by the size of the bars. Tubular metal resonators are mounted beneath the bars to amplify the sound. In the vibraphone the keys are metal, and rotating disks mounted in the resonators cause the pitch of each note to oscillate slightly.

distinctive noises when tapped. There were enough musical-sounding natural objects to give our prehistoric ancestors the idea of shaping solid objects to form musical instruments.

XYLOPHONES

A xylophone consists of wooden bars cut to precise lengths to give the desired notes when struck. Smaller bars make higher notes. An array of these bars mounted on a frame makes an instrument with a wide range of frequencies. Hollow gourds, again of carefully chosen sizes, may be hung beneath the bars to amplify the sound. In the modern xylophone metal tubes are often used as resonators.

SKINS AND MEMBRANES

Just as a stretched string makes a musical note when it is plucked, so a taut skin or other membrane makes a note when it

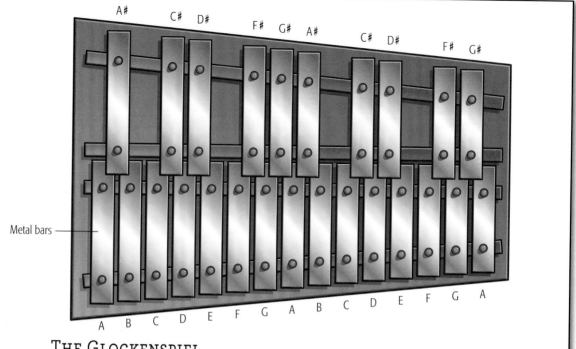

THE GLOCKENSPIEL

The glockenspiel consists of metal bars tuned a half-note apart. They are arranged like the keys of a piano, with the bars corresponding to the black piano keys in the upper row. Letters are note names.

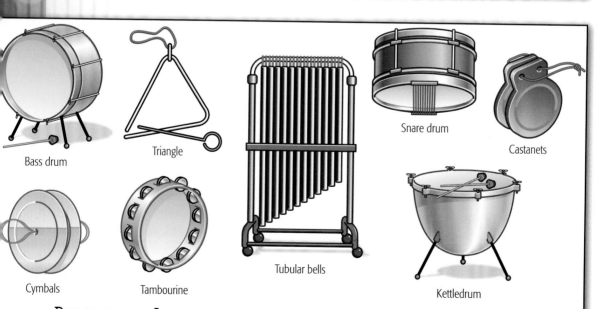

PERCUSSION INSTRUMENTS

Illustrated here are some of the huge family of instruments that are to be found in the percussion section of an orchestra.

is struck. If it is stretched over a hollow vessel, a loud, pleasing noise is produced. In many types of drum there is a mixture of many frequencies in the note, which does not have the pure sound of a plucked string. But some drums, such as the steel drums made from oil containers, are designed to be tuned precisely.

DRUMMING WITH TENSION

The note made by a drum depends not only on its size but also on the tension—the tautness—of the skin. The tighter the skin is, the higher the note. One traditional type of drum used in Africa and elsewhere has skin stretched over both ends by cords. The drum body has a "waist" so that the strings are clear of the body. The player holds the drum under one arm and squeezes the cage of cords while beating the drum with the other hand, creating a varying pitch.

A symphony orchestra usually has four or more tunable drums called kettledrums, often known by their Italian name of timpani. In the original type the drum's skin could be tightened (to raise the pitch of the note) or slackened (to lower the note) by turning keys mounted around the rim of the drum. In more modern kettledrums a foot pedal is used instead of keys to stretch or slacken the skin, which enables the pitch to be changed much more rapidly.

The pitch of a drum depends on its size. In orchestral drums, called timpani or kettledrums, the pitch can be varied by tightening the membrane, or skin, by means of a pedal.

Squeezing the cords on these drums changes the tension of the membranes and alters the pitch.

STRIKING METAL

When human beings first made metal objects, they discovered that they produced a satisfying clang when struck. That is because metals have a polycrystalline structure built from lattices of atoms that vibrate with very precise frequencies when they are struck. A maintenance engineer can judge the condition of a wheel on a train by hitting it with a hammer. A good wheel will produce a musical note, but a cracked wheel will make a dull, flat sound.

Though some bells are made of wood or pottery, most bells, and all large ones, are made of metal. The largest musical instruments of all are mighty church bells, made of bronze and weighing over 10 tons.

Priests at some temples in Asia summon worshippers to prayer by striking large gongs. They are usually cast or beaten out of bronze. Unlike a bell, a gong does not have a definite pitch but produces a mixture of tones. A cymbal is similar but is made from a disk of brass. Cymbals are often played in pairs to produce a metallic crashing sound when they are struck together.

This monk in Southeast Asia strikes a gong in celebration of Lao New Year.

CHAPTER SIX

TRAVELING AT THE SPEED OF SOUND

The fact that sound travels at a definite speed is easily noticed. The speed varies according to the medium in which the sound travels. Sound waves can be outpaced by jet planes, by space rockets during launch, and now even by jet-propelled cars.

Picture yourself in the middle of a thunderstorm. You see a lightning stroke 5 kilometers (3 miles) away. The light reaches you almost instantly—after about 1/60,000 of a second. But the sound, traveling at a speed of 1 kilometer every 3 seconds (1 mile every 5 seconds), takes 15 seconds to arrive.

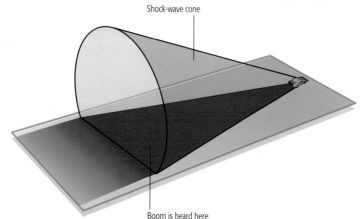

SUPERSONIC BOOM

When a jet-powered car driven by Andy Green took the world land-speed record at 1,228 kph (763 mph), spectators heard a supersonic boom. As the car sped forward, sound waves continually spread out from it. They piled up on a cone-shaped surface, forming a shock wave. In front of the shock wave the sound of the vehicle had not yet arrived. As the shock wave reached the listeners, they heard all the sound from a large stretch of the car's track simultaneously, creating the bang.

Shock-wave cone

Boom is heard here

You can see a delay even over shorter distances. The sound of a hammer blow 100 meters (330 feet) away is delayed by a noticeable one-third of a second from the sight of the hammer falling. (You never see this in movies. Directors always arrange for the boom of a distant explosion to coincide with the sight of it. They think their audience will be puzzled by a delay!)

The speed of sound in air increases with increases in temperature. At 0°C (32°F) it is 331.6 meters per second (1,088 feet per second) in dry air. At 20°C (68°F) it is 344 m/s (1,129 ft/s). The temperature of the atmosphere decreases up to an altitude of about 13 km, and so does the speed of sound. At this height the speed of sound falls to about 286 m/s (938 ft/s).

MACH SPEEDS

The ratio of the speed of an object to the speed of sound under the same circumstances is called its Mach number. Mach 1 is the speed of sound, Mach 2 is twice the speed of sound, and so on. The Mach

DOPPLER EFFECT

As the police car speeds toward a listening bystander, each sound wave has a shorter distance to travel to the listener than the previous one. The frequency is raised, and the sound rises in pitch. When the police car has passed by and is speeding away, the sound waves are stretched, their frequency is lowered, and the pitch of the siren falls.

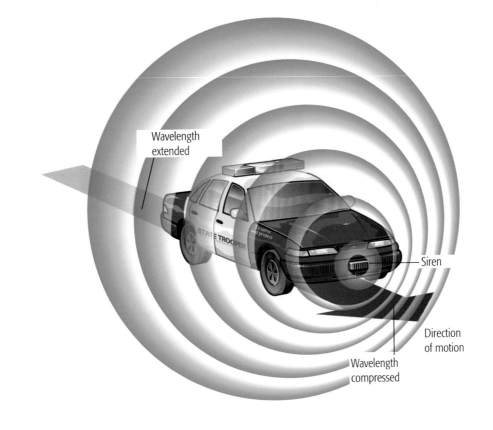

Wavelength extended

Siren

Direction of motion

Wavelength compressed

number is named after the Austrian physicist Ernst Mach.

Sound waves travel faster through liquids and solids. At sea a distant explosion will be heard twice—the first sound has traveled through water, and the second sound has traveled through air. The speed of sound in water is about four and a half times its speed in air.

CHRISTIAN DOPPLER

Christian Johann Doppler, born in 1803 in Salzburg, Austria, studied the wave motion of light and sound. In 1842 he showed how the apparent frequency and wavelength vary according to the motion of the source and the observer. When the source of the waves is approaching the observer, or vice versa, the apparent frequency increases. In the case of sound the pitch of the sound rises. In the case of light the colors of the light are shifted toward the short-wavelength blue colors. If the source and the observer are moving apart, the apparent frequency is lowered. Sound becomes deeper in pitch, while light becomes redder.

In 1845 Doppler was proved right. In a demonstration a locomotive pulled a carriage of trumpeters past some other musicians, who judged the change in pitch of the trumpet notes as the train passed them. Their judgments matched his predictions. Doppler died in 1853.

Supersonic jets are aircraft able to fly faster than the speed of sound. Most are used for scientific research and military purposes.

The sound of a moving ambulance's siren is an example of the Doppler effect. The pitch changes as the ambulance moves toward you and away from you.

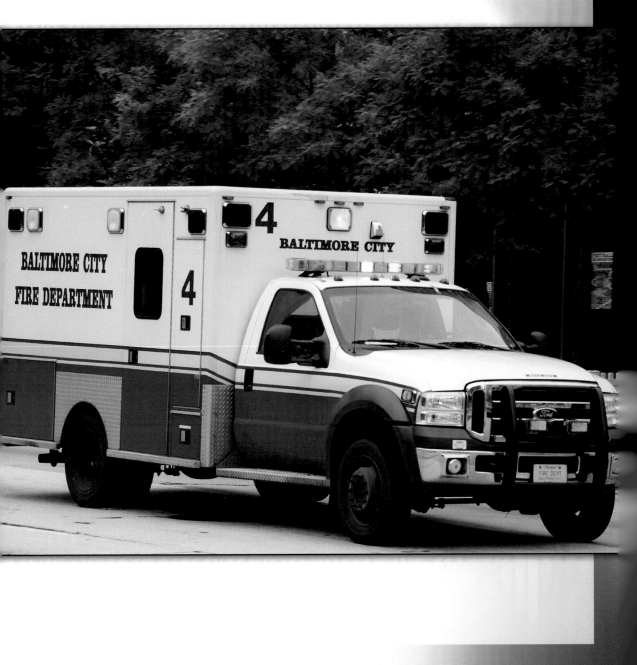

CHAPTER SEVEN

ULTRASONIC FREQUENCIES

We are surrounded by ultra-sound—sound so high-pitched that we cannot hear it. But animals can make these sounds and respond to them, and they fill the air and oceans with unheard cries. We make use of ultrasound in industry, warfare, and medicine.

Flesh is transparent to ultrasound, and doctors use ultrasound waves to peer inside our bodies. The deepest sounds we can hear consist of about 20 vibrations per second, or 20 hertz (named after the 19th-century German physicist Heinrich Hertz; its symbol is Hz). The highest audible frequency is about 20,000 Hz, or 20 kilohertz (1 kilohertz, symbol kHz, is 1,000 hertz).

Sound waves with frequencies higher than this are called "ultrasonic" or "supersonic." (This has nothing to do with supersonic speed: The speed of these waves is the same as that of sound with lower frequencies.)

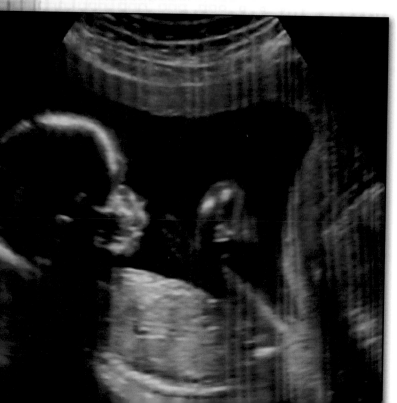

Ultrasound can be used to look into the human body. Because different sorts of tissue reflect and absorb the sound differently, a computer-generated picture of internal organs can be built up. Here a human fetus is seen in the womb.

This humpback whale communicates over huge distances by means of beautiful calls. The calls cover the full range of frequencies that we can hear, as well as subsonic and supersonic frequencies.

Many animals are able to hear this ultrasound. Dog whistles produce loud ultrasound, which dogs react to but which people cannot hear. Bats have an uncanny ability to find their way and hunt prey in darkness. They give out high-pitched squeaks at ultrasonic frequencies that can be as high as 200 kHz, and they detect the echoes from insects and other objects.

CREATING AND USING ULTRASOUND

The usual way of producing audible sound is through a loudspeaker (see chapter fourteen), in which a paper or metal diaphragm vibrates rapidly to create the sounds. But a diaphragm cannot be made to vibrate fast enough to produce ultrasound. Instead, the sound

Bats navigate using high-frequency sound as sonar. Most of the sound they produce is too high-pitched for us to hear. The bats' large and sensitive ears detect echoes, enabling the bats to home in on insects and avoid obstacles. So amazingly accurate is their navigational ability that bats can fly safely through darkened rooms crisscrossed by wires.

producer—called a transducer—employs a crystal that is made to vibrate by an oscillating electric current applied across its faces. The crystal is usually made of quartz or a chemical called Rochelle salt.

Ultrasound produced in this way is used for cleaning things. Clothing can be submerged in water or cleaning fluid and rapidly agitated to remove dirt by beaming in an ultrasound signal. Delicate machinery, such as a watch, can be cleaned in a similar way by using ultrasound.

UNDERWATER ULTRASOUND

The bats' method of navigation is also used by seafarers. Ultrasonic pulses sent out from ships are reflected from, for example, submarines, shoals of fish, or the seabed. The time the echo takes to return to the ship shows the distance of the object.

Now sonar is used in medicine. Ultrasound pulses can penetrate the human body, and the echoes from internal organs paint a picture of the body's interior.

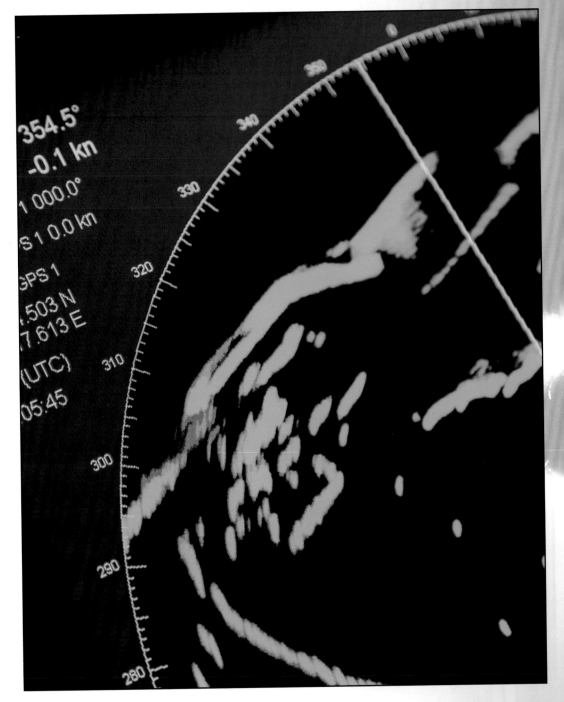

Submarines depend on sonar to "see" objects and obstacles in their path.

CHAPTER EIGHT

LOW AND SLOW FREQUENCIES

When sound vibrations are very slow, we do not perceive them as sound. But they can make themselves felt: They can shake buildings and cause destruction and death. An earthquake can set off vibrations that travel all the way through the planet.

The deep, low-frequency sounds from a church organ, or from a truck or plane, can make an entire building throb. In these cases, as well as the sounds we can hear there are vibrations that are of lower frequency. These vibrations are called infrasound, or subsonic sound. ("Subsonic" can also mean "slower than sound." In that sense it is applied to airplanes, for example.) Although human beings cannot hear infrasound, many animals can, among them whales and elephants.

Lower-frequency sounds travel farther than higher-frequency ones. That is why distant thunder is always deep and rumbling, while a nearby thunderclap is much sharper,

This sort of damage can be caused by an earthquake that shakes the ground for only a few moments and makes it move only a few centimeters.

with a cracking tone to it. Some animals take advantage of the long range of low-frequency sound. Whales emit infrasound to communicate over distances of as much as 160 km (100 miles). (Whales also make use of high-frequency ultrasound to communicate—see pages 34–37.)

In the 1980s naturalists discovered that elephants produce subsonic rumbling noises from their nasal passages. They use these sounds to communicate with one another over long distances.

RESONANCE

The throbbing that a deep sound makes is caused by a phenomenon called resonance. An object is said to resonate when it is made to vibrate by the vibration of some other nearby object. For example, sounding a single note near a piano—by plucking a guitar string, say—will cause the piano string that is tuned to the same note to vibrate. Other strings, such as those an octave higher or lower, will do the same.

Spiders are sensitive to subsonic vibrations. The trap-door spider, for example, hides in a burrow topped with a lid (the "trapdoor") that it has made. The spider can sense subsonic vibrations caused by the movement of an insect just outside the burrow. It flings open the trap-door, darts out, grabs its prey, and drags it into the burrow.

CHARLES RICHTER

The US seismologist Charles Francis Richter, who was born in 1900, will always be associated with the earthquake scale named after him. He devised it with another seismologist, Beno Gutenberg, over the years from 1927 to 1935. They rated the amount of energy released in an earthquake by the size of the marks made by the pen of a seismograph, with a correction for the distance of the earthquake from the observing laboratory. The points on the scale do not represent equal intervals. When you go from one point on the scale to the next, the energy released in the earthquake is multiplied by about 30. The scale has been revised several times as methods of measurement have improved. Richter died in 1985.

The vibrations of the air from the plucked string tend to make all the piano strings vibrate, but only those piano strings that naturally vibrate at the same frequency as the guitar string will develop a strong vibration. In a similar way, if someone pushing a child on a playground swing gives little pushes at just the same rate that the child is swinging, the movement of the swing will build up. Pushes at a different rate will be out of step with the regular motion of the swing,

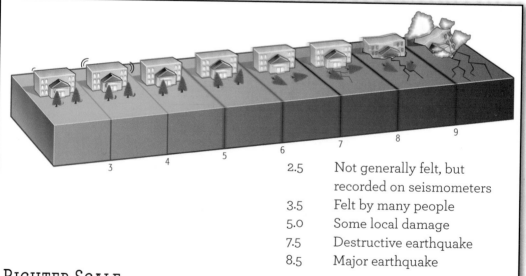

2.5	Not generally felt, but recorded on seismometers
3.5	Felt by many people
5.0	Some local damage
7.5	Destructive earthquake
8.5	Major earthquake

RICHTER SCALE

The energy released in an earthquake is described by the numbers on the Richter scale. The amount of damage caused by the earthquake depends not only on its magnitude on the Richter scale but also on its depth and on the numbers of people and buildings in the area. Another scale, the Mercalli scale, rates earthquarkes according to their visible effects.

and this motion will be prevented from building up.

Buildings and furniture do not usually resonate to normal sound frequencies. Because the natural rates of vibration of these objects are low, they resonate (if they resonate at all) to infrasound. A church or concert hall can be damaged over the years by the deep notes from an organ.

A spectacular example of harmful resonance occurred in 1940, when the Tacoma Narrows suspension bridge in Tacoma, Washington, started to vibrate uncontrollably, set in motion by the wind. The deck of the bridge snaked like a shaken rope, flinging cars into the river below and finally collapsing. Since that disaster new bridges have always incorporated antiresonance features.

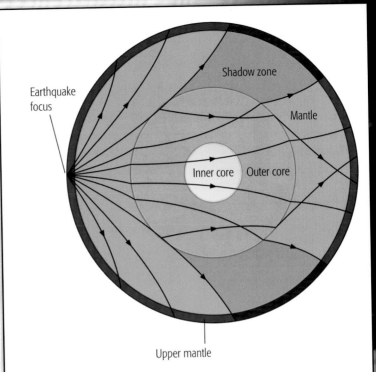

THE SHAKING EARTH

Earthquake waves reveal the inner structure of the Earth. Because they travel at different speeds in different layers, they are bent when they pass from one layer to the next. The shadow zone, in which no S waves are felt, reveals the existence of the outer core. P waves pass through the core. More information is provided by the different times of arrival of shock waves.

VIBRATING EARTH

Most earthquakes are caused by shifts within the top 300 km (about 200 miles) of the Earth's mantle. The shifts are small, but affect enormous quantities of rock. The shifts cause vibrations of all frequencies in the surrounding crust. Some vibrations travel for large distances through the crust, others through the deeper parts of the Earth—the mantle and core. Earthquake vibrations are the sound of a whole planet being shaken.

STUDYING AND MEASURING EARTHQUAKES

Sound waves in a solid, unlike sound waves in a fluid such as water or air, can be of two kinds. In one, atoms and

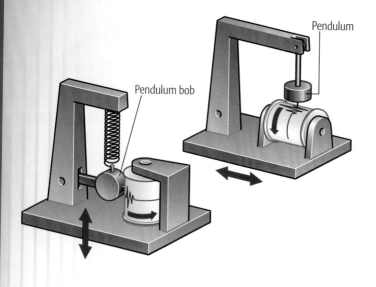

Pendulum

Pendulum bob

SEISMOGRAPHS

A seismograph designed to detect vertical movements of the ground has a pendulum bob suspended from a spring, so that the bob can bounce up and down (left). Horizontal movements are detected by a seismograph with a pendulum that is free to swing from side to side (right).

molecules are made to vibrate backward and forward in the same direction as the motion of the wave. This is the same as the movement of the particles in a sound wave in a gas or liquid. But in the other kind of sound wave in a solid the atoms or molecules move from side to side. These waves are like the waves you can send along a rope that is fixed at one end by shaking its free end.

In the study of earthquakes the side-to-side waves are called S (shear) waves, and the faster, pressure waves are called P waves. The different conditions of pressure, density, and rock composition at different depths below the surface of the

Earth also affect the speeds of both S waves and P waves.

The varying conditions in the body of the planet cause the paths of earthquake waves (known as seismic waves) to bend. The pattern of waves arriving at different places around the world following an earthquake is very complex, but over many years they have been disentangled to reveal a lot about the structure of the Earth. They reveal a difference between the lighter rocks of the thin crust and the denser rocks of the mantle, which extends halfway toward the center. And they show that there is a liquid core of molten iron and nickel that the S waves cannot penetrate. There is also an inner-most solid iron–nickel core.

When a tremor is felt in a particular spot, the ground generally moves both from side to side and up and down. Seismographs, or Earth-tremor measuring devices, record these tremors as graphs, traditionally on paper. The instrument consists of a pendulum, which has a heavy weight or bob, that is free either to bounce up and down on a spring or to swing from side to side. The bob carries a pen that makes a trace on paper mounted on a revolving drum. The heavy bob tends to stay still, while the rest of the instrument shakes during a tremor, producing the wavy trace. Nowadays the information is often recorded electronically as computer data rather than as an ink trace.

In March 2011 an earthquake occurred off the coast of Japan. The vibrations caused a tsunami, or series of waves, which swept over Japan's coast. About 28,700 people were killed.

CHAPTER NINE

MEASURING LOUDNESS

Human hearing is incredibly sensitive. A person who has normal hearing will have no difficulty in hearing a person next to them who is talking in a normal conversational tone. Yet he or she is emitting only one ten-thousandth as much energy as is given out by an ordinary 100-watt lightbulb.

Scientists measure loudness of sounds in terms of a unit called the decibel (symbol dB). The decibel equals one-tenth of another unit called the bel, named for Alexander Graham Bell, inventor of the telephone, but the larger unit is hardly ever used. A difference of 10 dB corresponds to a ratio in loudness of 10 times. That is, the intensity of a sound of 70 dB is 10 times that of a sound of 60 dB. The sound level in a busy city street is typically around 70 dB. In a club or a rock concert the sound level is around 110 dB. A supersonic fighter taking off 500 meters (550 yards) away puts out an ear-splitting 120 dB.

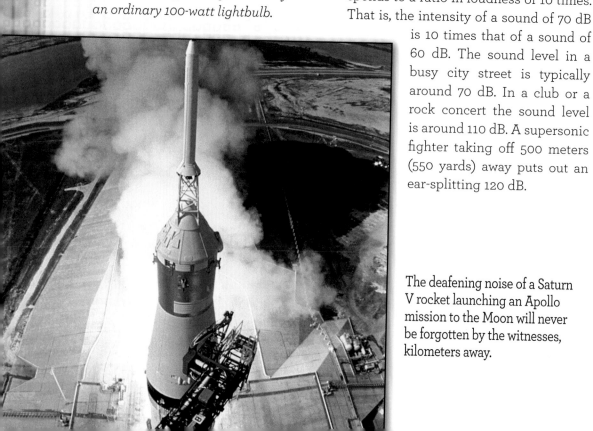

The deafening noise of a Saturn V rocket launching an Apollo mission to the Moon will never be forgotten by the witnesses, kilometers away.

The loudness of a sound wave is related to its energy. This energy, in turn, depends on the mass of air molecules set in motion by a vibrating object. The larger the mass of air, the louder the sound. For example, the vibrating diaphragm in the earpiece of a telephone is too small to vibrate a large mass of air, so it cannot produce loud sounds. But the diaphragms in a rock band's large loudspeakers can pump out more than 110 dB.

LIMITING EXPOSURE

The levels of noise in modern life has become a major source of concern. Physicians now know that years of exposure to loud noise can cause severe deafness in later life. Government regulations restrict the amount of noise to which workers can be exposed. Ear protectors, which are worn like headphones to shut out noise, must be worn in many jobs, such as operating a jackhammer or when practicing with firearms. The flight paths of airliners near airports are controlled to minimize noise nuisance to local residents.

DEGREES OF LOUDNESS

Loudness is measured in decibels (dB). The faintest sound that can be heard by the average person is defined as being 0 dB. At 130 dB, which is a trillion times louder than the faintest sounds that can be heard, noise begins to be painful to the person hearing it.

Pain threshold

Hearing threshold

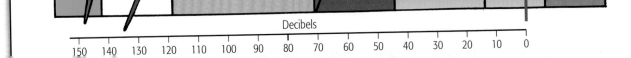

Decibels

150   140   130   120   110   100   90   80   70   60   50   40   30   20   10   0

CHAPTER TEN

REFLECTIONS AND ECHOES

Even in total darkness we can sense the presence of objects around us. This ability is largely due to our subconscious perceptions of sounds reflected by objects. The principle of reflection of sound is used in sonar to detect objects under water.

Sound waves, like all other types of wave, can be reflected. They can be reflected by solid objects, by the surface of water, and even by the boundary between layers of water that are at different temperatures beneath the surface. A reflected sound is called an echo.

An echo from a distant object is noticeably delayed compared with the original sound. When you shout or clap your hands to hear the echo, every 3 seconds' delay represents 1 kilometer (5 seconds represents 1 mile). To figure out the distance of the object that is reflecting the sound, you have to divide the

The submerged wreck of a ship is clearly revealed in this sonar image.

delay time by two, because the sound has traveled both ways by the time you hear the echo.

ECHOES AND ACOUSTICS

Echoes from nearby objects are not obvious, but they do affect the quality of all the sounds we hear. A radio program made in the open air sounds quite different from one made indoors, where there are echoes from walls and ceilings. The sounds in a huge cathedral are very different from those in a small kitchen. A room echoes when it is empty of people and of soft furnishings, such as drapes and upholstered chairs, which absorb a great deal of the sound. The characteristics of the sound inside a room or building are called its acoustics.

Reflected wave

Outgoing sound wave

MAKING ECHOES

You hear an echo of your own voice when some of its sound energy is reflected from an object and returned to you. A rocky cliff or the wall of a building makes good echoes.

Multiple echoes can be confusing. For example, somebody listening to a speaker but sitting toward the back of a large hall hears sounds coming to them by several

FISHING WITH SOUND

Sonar is of huge importance to the fishing industry. Even small fishing vessels search for shoals of fish with sonar. From the trace on the sonar screen an experienced operator can judge the size of the shoal and can often tell what type of fish it is.

routes, but not all at exactly the same time. In addition to the sound of the speaker's voice arriving directly, sounds also arrive a fraction of a second later after having been reflected from the walls and from the ceiling. This mixture of sounds distorts the speaker's voice. Such reflections can be avoided by covering the walls and ceilings with sound-absorbent materials, such as tiles made from foamed plastics. In a well-designed theater or concert hall the tip-up seats absorb about the same amount of sound as does a person sitting in them. As a result, the hall has the same acoustic properties even when many of the seats are empty.

Researchers use sonar and handheld devices to study and map parts of Port Royal, Jamaica, that were destroyed and submerged underwater after devastating earthquakes.

The Musikverein, in Vienna, Austria, is considered one of the best concert halls in the world because of its great acoustics.

CHAPTER ELEVEN

SOUND AND WEATHER

Sounds can sometimes be strangely elusive. Conversations can be difficult out of doors. Yet at other times sounds carry well over long distances. One reason for this variation is that temperature and windspeed can vary with height above the ground.

The paths of sound waves can be gently bent as well as sharply reflected. Sound waves, like other waves, usually bend when their speed changes.

For example, sound slows down when it enters cooler air. Normally, air high up is cooler than air near the ground. Sound waves rising at an angle to the horizontal from a source on the ground are slowed as they rise. The braking effect drags them around so that they are bent upward. (This is rather like a column of soldiers marching at an angle onto rough ground that slows them down. They tend to deviate from the direction they were marching in.)

This bending upward tends to reduce the loudness of the sound at ground level

Fog horns were often used to warn ships they were near the shore. Today, modern navigational tools have made most fog horns unnecessary.

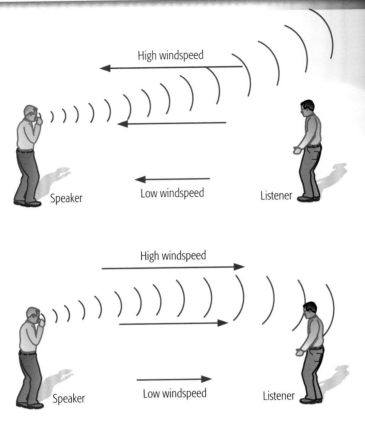

HEARING AND THE WIND

Windspeed usually increases with height. Higher above the ground sound waves going upwind are slowed down. All the sound waves going in that direction are therefore bent upward. They are hard to hear at ground level. Higher-altitude sound waves going downwind are speeded up and bent downward, making them easier to hear.

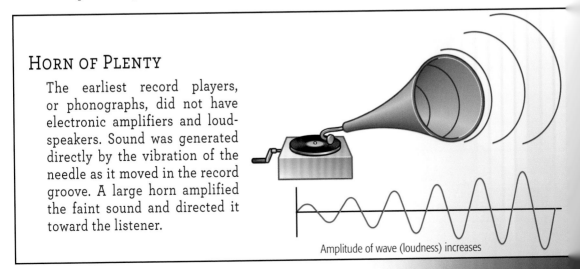

HORN OF PLENTY

The earliest record players, or phonographs, did not have electronic amplifiers and loudspeakers. Sound was generated directly by the vibration of the needle as it moved in the record groove. A large horn amplified the faint sound and directed it toward the listener.

Amplitude of wave (loudness) increases

some distance from the source. In the open air sounds are weaker at a distance than they would be in air of uniform temperature.

The effects can be the reverse when air is warmer higher up than it is near the ground. This happens in certain weather conditions and is common in the polar regions, where the air is chilled near the frozen ground. Sound waves are speeded up as they rise, and this makes them swerve downward. It is then often possible to hear quiet sounds over great distances.

The electronic amplifier in the bullhorn makes the speaker's words louder, but the shaping of the horn is also important in ensuring that the sound goes toward the crowd he is addressing and is not wasted.

FOCUSING SOUND

The wind also affects audibility for a similar reason. Windspeed normally increases with height, and the effect of this is to make any sound waves traveling upwind bend upward, and any sound waves traveling downwind bend downward. This makes it easier to hear people speaking, for example, when they are upwind.

Sounds can be made easier to hear if they are focused into a beam. They are stronger within the beam and weaker anywhere outside the beam.

A loudspeaker, an old-fashioned phonograph, and a bullhorn all have a horn whose shape is designed to reflect sound waves into a limited beam, rather than spreading them outward in all directions.

Speakers often use microphones to amplify
their voices when speaking outside.

CHAPTER TWELVE

HUMAN HEARING

Our ears give us knowledge of the world of sounds around us. The complex analysis of sounds, telling us what frequencies are present in them, takes place in hidden structures within the head.

Our sense of balance happens to be located in the same structures. Most defects of hearing, apart from total deafness, can be corrected by physicians.

Human beings detect sound by means of a marvelously complex sensory mechanism. The visible flaps of skin that we call ears, and anatomists call pinnas or pinnae, are only the outermost part of a structure that goes deep into the head. This structure is divided into the outer, middle, and inner ears.

We can keep our balance, sense which way up we are, and judge how our body is moving thanks to the semicircular canals, organs in the inner ear.

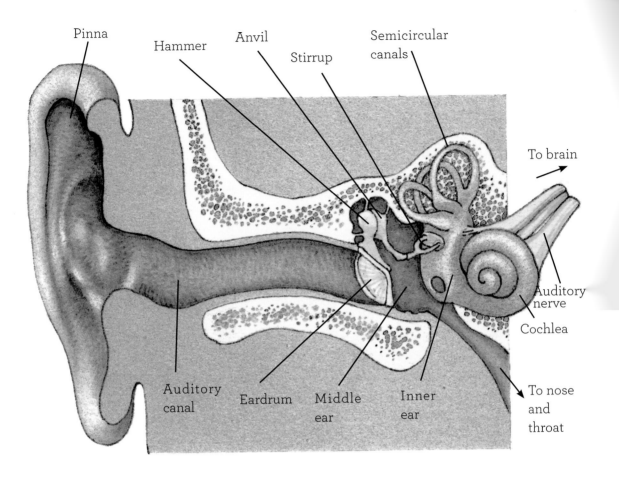

Pinna
Hammer
Anvil
Stirrup
Semicircular canals
To brain
Auditory nerve
Cochlea
Auditory canal
Eardrum
Middle ear
Inner ear
To nose and throat

INSIDE THE EAR

The pinna, or ear-flap, is shaped to give us information about the direction from which a sound comes. Sound waves are channeled along the auditory canal, making the eardrum vibrate. Beyond the eardrum is the middle ear, which is connected to the nose and throat. The vibrations of the eardrum are passed along three bones joined together, called the hammer (malleus), anvil (incus), and stirrup (stapes). The movement of the stirrup sets up vibrations in the fluid-filled inner ear. Hairlike cells in the coiled tube of the cochlea send electrical signals to the brain. The three fluid-filled semicircular canals detect head movements.

A tuning fork gives out a tone of a single frequency. Such sounds are almost unknown in nature. Because of distortions in the ear and nervous system, we often think we can perceive other frequencies in what is really a perfectly pure tone.

Sounds from the outside world pass down a passage called the auditory canal and make the eardrum vibrate (see the illustration on page 55). These vibrations are passed through a chain of three small bones to a complicated fluid-filled structure in the inner ear called the cochlea. The vibrations of the fluid in turn cause small, fine cells called hair cells to vibrate, generating electrical signals. The signals travel to the brain, and a sound is perceived. The deepest, longest-wavelength sounds travel farthest along the cochlea; so when hairs in that far part of the cochlea vibrate, the brain can "work out" that there are low frequencies in the sound that has been heard.

MOVEMENTS AND BALANCE

Our sense of balance is also controlled from the inner ear, where there are three fluid-filled loops called the semicircular canals at right angles to one another. Movements of the head set the fluid in the canals in motion, providing information from which the brain can compute the position and movement of the head in relation to the direction of gravity. Dizziness is caused by the fluid in the canals continuing to move after the head has stopped moving.

PROBLEMS WITH HEARING

Various things can upset the delicate hearing mechanism, with results that vary from hardness of hearing to profound deafness. The simplest cause of partial deafness is an obstruction in the auditory canal, most often by earwax, which is easily removed by a physician. Inflammation of the middle ear (otitis) is another possible cause that can usually be treated successfully. More difficult to remedy are problems with the ear's sound-detecting apparatus, the auditory nerve, or the brain's hearing center. A hearing aid may help; an alternative is a cochlear implant, in which audio signals are fed to an electrode placed in the inner ear.

Because they do not clearly hear sounds, people who are deaf or hard of hearing use their hands and facial expressions to communicate.

CHAPTER THIRTEEN

THE VIBRATING HUMAN VOICE

The human voice is astonishingly complex and flexible. Subtle, controlled movements of the jaws, tongue, lips, teeth, and vocal cords together produce the countless different types of vocal sound.

Children master this control in the first few years of life, but scientists are still patiently uncovering the intricacies of human speech.

The human voice works like a combination of a wind instrument and a stringed instrument. It is produced by air from the lungs blowing between two organs called the vocal cords. They are housed in the larynx, or voicebox, which is located at the front of the throat and at

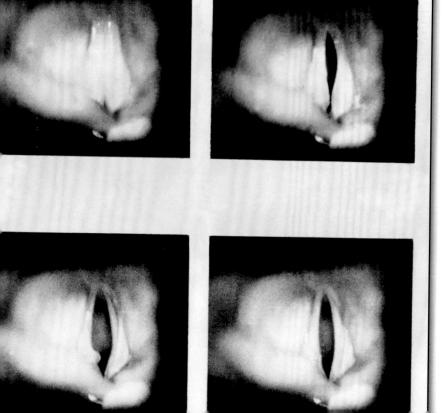

In this view down a person's throat the vocal cords are the V-shaped organs in the center, located in the larynx. Air passing through them from the lungs makes them vibrate.

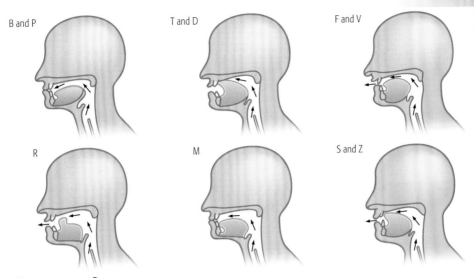

SHAPING SOUNDS

Mouth movements that produce some of the consonant sounds are shown here. B and P, for example, are called plosive because the lips are pressed together and then parted, releasing air explosively. T and D are called alveolar, because the tongue is briefly pressed against the alveolus, the front of the roof of the mouth. Other sounds are classified similarly.

the top of the windpipe, or trachea (see the illustration on page 60).

The vocal cords form a V shape across the windpipe. They are made of elastic tissue and can be pulled by muscles in the larynx. When the muscles are relaxed, the vocal cords are relatively far apart, and no sound is made by air passing through. The muscles can move the cords together, and then they vibrate as air passes between them. The muscles can also tighten the cords, raising the pitch, or loosen them to lower the pitch.

At puberty there are changes in the larynx. Boys' vocal cords generally become less tightly stretched, so that the pitch of the voice drops.

The epiglottis is part of the larynx. This flap of cartilage closes off the top of the windpipe when we swallow so that food cannot enter the windpipe and perhaps choke us. The food is diverted into the esophagus, or gullet, the tube that leads to the stomach.

VOICED AND UNVOICED

Some sounds are made without the vocal cords vibrating. They are called unvoiced, and include the P and T sounds. The B and D sounds, by contrast, are made with vibration of the vocal cords and are described as voiced. Voiced sounds also include all the vowels.

The sounds generated in the larynx are modified in the mouth. We make complex movements of the tongue, lips, and teeth to form the vowel and consonant sounds of speech. Tongue and lip positions are shown for some consonants in the diagram above.

There is a wide range of frequencies in human speech. The ability to detect high frequencies is important in distinguishing many of the consonants from one another. The commonest forms of deafness that develop as people get older involve difficulty in distinguishing sounds in this way.

FINGERPRINT OF THE VOICE

There are individual differences in the mix of frequencies in different people's voices, even when speaking the same words. These frequencies can be electronically analyzed and represented in an image called a voiceprint. A voiceprint can be used to identify the speaker with the same certainty with which a fingerprint can identify an individual. A recording of a nuisance telephone call can be turned into a voiceprint that can be compared with the voiceprint of a suspect.

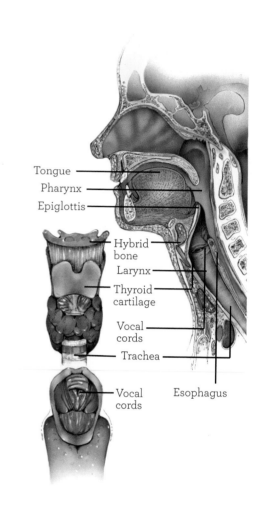

Tongue
Pharynx
Epiglottis
Hybrid bone
Larynx
Thyroid cartilage
Vocal cords
Trachea
Vocal cords
Esophagus

MACHINERY OF SPEECH

The vocal cords are housed in a container called the larynx, at the top of the windpipe, or trachea, which lies at the front of the throat. When speaking, a person blows air through the vocal cords while altering their position and tension to vary the pitch of the sounds produced. Movements of the mouth make further alterations in the sounds to produce recognizable speech.

The tone and frequency of a human voice helps us distinguish between the voices of friends and strangers.

CHAPTER FOURTEEN

RECORDING AND PLAYING SOUNDS

Nothing seems more elusive than a sound, which vanishes in a moment. Yet we have learned to store sounds, send them around the world, make them loud or soft at will, and mold them as if they were clay. With modern technology the vocal and instrumental sounds made by performers are now just raw material for the sound engineer.

The first sound recordings consisted of grooves in a wax surface whose shape was a direct imitation of the shape of waves of sound. They were made in 1877 by the American inventor Thomas Alva Edison, using his phonograph. A person would speak or sing loudly in front of the large end of a horn, and the sound was focused to make a metal plate vibrate. A needle attached to the plate cut a wavy groove into the soft surface of a revolving wax-coated cylinder.

To play back the sound, practically the same equipment was used in reverse. The

Miniaturization has made it possible to hear the music of your choice anywhere using a radio, CD player, or MP3 player.

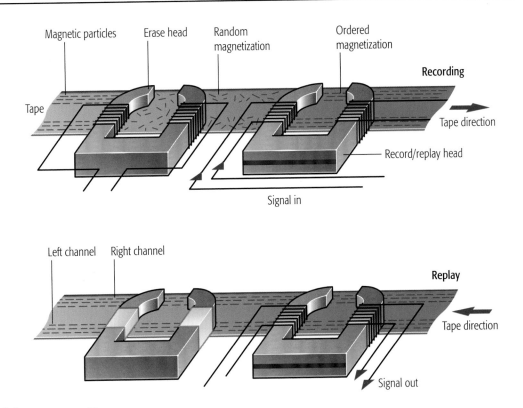

Magnetic particles · Erase head · Random magnetization · Ordered magnetization · Recording · Tape · Tape direction · Record/replay head · Signal in

Left channel · Right channel · Replay · Tape direction · Signal out

MAGNETIC RECORDING

During recording the erase head uses magnetic fields to remove any signal already on the tape. The record head then magnetizes the tape in a pattern that corresponds to the original sound. When played back, the twin tracks of magnetization cause electrical signals to be generated in the read head, one for each stereo channel.

cylinder rotated, making a needle in the groove vibrate. The needle was attached to a plate, which also vibrated, reproducing a faint version of the original sound, which was amplified by a large horn.

Discs were soon found to be lighter and more convenient than cylinders. The first 78 rpm records were made from a type of resin called shellac. Vinyl, a type of plastic, was used for 33 rpm and 45 rpm records from the 1950s onward.

USING ELECTRONICS

Sound recording was much improved when electronic microphones and loudspeakers were developed. Electronic microphones generate electric currents varying in strength, representing the varying intensity (loudness) of the sound from moment to moment. This signal controls the cutting of the original disc.

When a vinyl disc is played back, the vibrations of the stylus (pickup head) are converted into an electric signal, which is used to drive a loudspeaker (see the illustration on page 66).

MAGNETS AND METALS

Recording on vinyl discs achieved superb quality, but was difficult to do outside the studio. Magnetic tape recording could be carried out to a reasonable standard by amateurs, and the equipment eventually became portable and convenient.

A magnetic recording tape consists of a plastic film coated with metallic particles. They become magnetized when exposed to a strong magnetic field. During recording the tape is wound past two electromagnets. An electromagnet consists of a wire carrying an electric current wrapped around a metal core. The current creates a magnetic field, which the metal core increases. So the whole device is a controllable magnet.

The first electromagnet in a tape recorder is called the erase head, and its job is to remove any existing

COMPACT DISC

In the underside of a CD, or compact disc, are etched billions of tiny pits, arranged in a spiral track. There are also regions, called flats, where there are no pits. The CD player's read head swings between the center and the edge of the disc as the disc spins. A laser beam (red) is shone onto the disc, and its reflections are sensed. The long sequence of pits and flats is thus translated into a stream of electronic signals. They in turn are converted into sound in the loudspeakers.

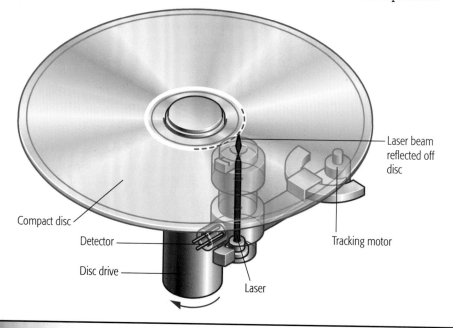

Compact disc
Detector
Disc drive
Laser
Laser beam reflected off disc
Tracking motor

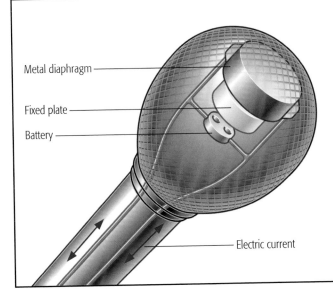

Metal diaphragm

Fixed plate

Battery

Electric current

MICROPHONE

A microphone generates a pattern of electric signals that is the same as the pattern of the waves in the sound. In the microphone shown here, the sound wave makes the metal diaphragm vibrate. The varying distance between the diaphragm and a fixed metal plate generates a varying voltage, which is passed to an amplifier.

magnetization on the tape. The second electromagnet is called the record/ replay head. A varying current flows through it, representing the sound being recorded.

This creates a varying magnetic field, and it in turn magnetizes the metal coating on the tape. A pattern of strong and weak magnetization is put onto the tape.

This control room is next door to a soundproofed recording studio. The main job of the banks of computerized instruments in the control room is to mix the dozens of different tracks, which are separate recordings of the session made by different microphones.

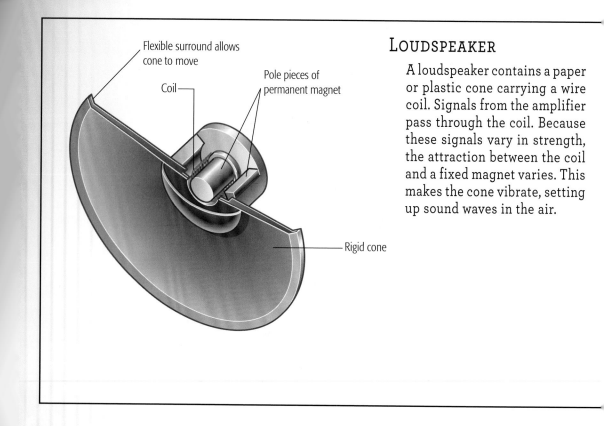

Flexible surround allows cone to move

Coil

Pole pieces of permanent magnet

Rigid cone

LOUDSPEAKER

A loudspeaker contains a paper or plastic cone carrying a wire coil. Signals from the amplifier pass through the coil. Because these signals vary in strength, the attraction between the coil and a fixed magnet varies. This makes the cone vibrate, setting up sound waves in the air.

During playback the tape is wound past the record/playback head. The changing magnetic field generates a changing electrical signal in the head, which is converted into sound.

GOING DIGITAL

The wavy shape of the groove in a vinyl disc is just like a picture of the sound wave. The compact disc, or CD, is a digital device, storing information about the sound in the form of a sequence of numbers (digits). It consists of a plastic-coated aluminum disc in which a track consisting of tiny pits about 0.6 of a micrometer (24 millionths of an inch) across spirals outward from the center.

At each position along the track a pit may be present or may be lacking. These two possibilities represent the two digits 0 and 1. Combinations of two digits are enough to represent any number in binary code.

The science of recording and reproducing sound has come a long way since the end of the 19th century.

Each group of 16 digits represents any number from 0 to 65,535. This corresponds to the loudness of the sound at any one moment. Just over 44,000 such groups stream from the CD pickup head every second (along with many more digits representing various kinds of error-checking and control information). Sampling a sound over 44,000 times per second is enough to represent it with an accuracy far surpassing what any other method of sound recording can achieve.

A new digital medium called MP3 was introduced in the 1990s. It compresses music by leaving out sounds that we do not normally hear, such as those above 16 kHz (the upper threshold of human hearing). MP3 is popular on the Internet since it enables tracks to be downloaded quickly.

Many people now download music directly from the Internet to their home computers, tablets, and smart phones.

CHAPTER FIFTEEN

BIOGRAPHY: ALEXANDER GRAHAM BELL

Alexander Graham Bell is best known as the inventor of the telephone, though he worked on many other ideas during his lifetime, including the electric telegraph, a "photophone," hydrofoils, and airplanes. He began investigating ways of producing mechanical speech while working as a speech therapist, teaching deaf people in Boston, Massachusetts. His "speaking telephone" would transform conmmunications throughout the world.

Alexander Graham Bell was born into the talking business. His grandfather taught elocution (the art of clear public speaking) in London, while his father, Melville Bell, invented a system of writing down speech that he called "Visible Speech." Unlike modern methods that indicate sounds (phonetics), Melville Bell's approach used diagrams to show the positions of the tongue, teeth, and lips during speech. This was intended to make it particularly suitable for teaching deaf people to speak. Alexander also would later direct his work to helping deaf people.

Alexander Graham Bell forever changed the way people communicate over distances.

KEY DATES

1847	Born March 2 in Edinburgh, Scotland
1870	The family emigrates to Canada
1871	Teaches deaf people in Boston, Massachusetts
1873	Appointed professor of vocal physiology at Boston University
1875	Obtains patent for first transmission of sound by telephone
1877	Bell Telephone Company established; marries Mabel Hubbard
1878	Daughter Elsie May is born
1880	Daughter Marian (Daisy) is born; Volta Laboratory set up
1881	Infant son, Edward, dies
1882	Bell becomes Canadian citizen
1883	Infant son, Robert, dies
1886	Establishes Volta Bureau as center of study into deafness
1897	Elected president of the National Geographic Society
1915	Takes part in opening of first transcontinental telephone line
1922	August 2, Bell dies at Cape Breton Island, Nova Scotia, Canada

Father and son developed an impressive parlor game that never failed to amaze. Melville would invite a foreigner to speak in a language unknown to both of the Bells. He would record the passage in Visible Speech and then summon Alexander who would, without understanding a word he was saying, read back the passage with near-perfect pronunciation.

Alexander was born in Edinburgh, Scotland, the second of three sons. He attended school on and off until he was 14, but his education was largely gained at home. After spending a year in London in 1862, Alexander returned to Scotland and taught music and elocution at Weston House Academy in Elgin; he later taught in Bath, England.

In 1868 he moved to London, and began work as his father's assistant. In 1870 his older brother Melville died, aged 25, of the lung disease tuberculosis that had killed his younger brother two years previously; shocked and distressed by the loss of both his brothers, Alexander himself became sick. He and his parents emigrated to Canada, which was thought to be a particularly healthy place to live. While Alexander recovered, Melville began at once to lecture on his Visible Speech system.

The Boston School for the Deaf was interested in adopting the system, and in 1871 the staff there invited Melville to show them how it worked. He sent Alexander instead, who quickly established a practice in Boston working

PRIZES AND PATRONAGE

Bell was an enthusiastic patron. In 1880 he was awarded the Volta Prize by the French government for his invention of the telephone; he used the prize money to set up the Volta Laboratory for scientific research in Washington, D.C. Bell also cofounded publication of *Science*, later the official journal of the American Association for the Advancement of Science. As president of the National Geographic Society, he was convinced that pictures were the best means of showing the world to people who could not travel, and helped develop the society's journal into the visual feast that became famous worldwide.

Bell's lifelong interest in helping the deaf led him to set up the Volta Bureau as a center for studies on the subject, and to found the American Association to Promote the Teaching of Speech to the Deaf (renamed the Alexander Graham Bell Association for the Deaf in 1956). In 1887 he met Helen Keller (1880–1968). She had become blind and deaf at 19 months old, and Bell found a teacher who was able to teach her to speak. In 1893 the 13-year-old Keller (later to become a famous writer and lecturer) ceremonially opened the new Volta Bureau building.

After his death, Bell's name was given to one of the world's most important scientific institutions, the Bell Laboratories. Known more familiarly as the Bell Lab, it was founded in 1925 with a staff of 3,000 and located in Murray Hill, New Jersey. By 1983 the Bell Lab had been granted 20,000 patents and its staff had been awarded seven Nobel prizes.

HELEN KELLER AND
ALEXANDER GRAHAM BELL

WHOSE IDEA WAS IT ANYWAY?

Bell had offered to sell his patents to the powerful Western Union telegraph company in 1876, but they rejected the offer. Without a buyer, Bell assigned the patents to his father-in-law, Gardiner Hubbard. By the time the Bell Telephone Company had been established in 1877, the first of many legal challenges had been issued against Bell.

In the United States the rights to inventions go to whoever first had the idea (in most other countries they go to whoever files the patent first). For this reason there can be a tendency in the United States for unknown inventors to "discover" old notebooks in order to prove they were the first to come up with the device.

Over a period of 18 years there were some 600 challenges to Bell's patents. Some of these were fraudulent and supported by forged documents. Others were little more than blackmail, threatening endless nuisance and lawsuits unless the petitioner was paid off. However, the most famous of the lawsuits involving Bell's telephone was launched by the Bell Telephone Company against Western Union (who had of course turned down the patents) and Elisha Gray, who had filed a rival patent. The two sides finally reached an agreement, and the *Boston Daily Advertiser* of October 25, 1879, reported that "the rival and conflicting interests in the various telephone patents have at last been harmonized, and Professor Bell is master of the field...."

PATENTLY PROFITABLE

There was good reason for people to want to own Bell's patents. As the *Boston Daily Advertiser* noted after the patent verdict, "The Bell telephone has a future of fame and fortune in store for it not surpassed by any of the great discoveries of our time." The growth of the telephone business was indeed phenomenal. As early as 1878 the first telephone exchange switchboard was operating in New Haven, Connecticut. By the end of the century there were more than a million phones in the United States, a figure that had grown to 186 million a century later.

The challenges continued throughout the lifetime of the patents, but Bell won every case. By 1883 the stock he held in the companies that owned his patents had made him a millionaire.

with deaf people, and by 1873 had been appointed professor of vocal physiology at Boston University.

EXPERIMENTS WITH SOUND

Much of Bell's early experimental work concerned developing devices to help deaf people to communicate. He first tried to make what he called a "phonautograph," which aimed to convert speech into written sound patterns. In this way deaf people could easily check their own speech. In the course of developing his new machine, Bell experimented with various types of membrane, including a real human eardrum, in order to try to imitate the way it worked. The eardrum is a thin, semitransparent, pliable structure: how, he wondered, could such a membrane move the solid bones of the inner ear? If a thin membrane could do such

Bell is seen here, in the center, with his family, including his wife, Mabel, and two grown daughters.

heavy work, might it not also respond to sound waves by somehow modifying the flow of an electric current?

Initial experiments were unsuccessful, however. Bell was able to take his work further only because Gardiner Greene Hubbard, a wealthy Boston attorney who had interests in the electric telegraph, now stepped in with an offer to finance him. Hubbard's daughter Mabel had been made deaf at the age of five by an attack of scarlet fever. She was a pupil of Bell's, and Hubbard was so impressed by his efforts on her behalf that he agreed to back him. Mabel later (in 1877) became Bell's wife.

ELECTRIC SPEECH

Bell did not set out to invent the telephone. He had originally begun trying to develop a "harmonic" or "multiple telegraph," a device that could receive several telegraph messages at once. By late 1874 he had taken on as an assistant a young mechanic and model-maker named Thomas Watson (1854–1934). Together they began work on trying to develop another idea of Bell's: a device that would be able to transmit speech using electricity.

The principles behind Bell's and all other work in this field derive from the researches of Danish physicist Hans Christian Oersted (1777–1851), and English chemist and physicist Michael Faraday (1791–1867). In 1820 Oersted discovered that, if he passed an electric current through a wire, it generated a magnetic field around it. In 1831 Faraday proved that disturbances in this magnetic field can generate an electric current, whose strength depends on how much the magnetic field is disturbed. This is known as "induction;" it produces an "induced" current.

A tuning fork consists of two metal prongs. When these are struck, they vibrate to produce a note of an exact pitch. Bell's basic idea was to link a tuning fork to an electromagnet. The strength of the current induced by the electromagnet depended on the pitch of the vibrating tuning fork. This current could then flow through a wire to a second electromagnet and produce in a second tuning fork the same note as the first. Bell hoped that several forks tuned to different frequencies might be used to send different messages at the same time.

SUCCESSFUL TRANSMISSION

The breakthrough came in June 1875, when Watson was in one room and Bell in another. Vibrating reeds had taken the

Michael Faraday (1791–1867) was a major influence and innovator in the study of electricity.

THOMAS AUGUSTUS WATSON 1854-1934

Bell first met Watson in 1874 when he was working as a mechanic in a local work-shop. Watson was recommended to Bell as an assistant. They worked together for several years; after their work on developing the telephone Watson was given a 10 percent interest in the original Bell company, and Bell himself was awarded a 30 percent interest.

After leaving Bell in 1881 Watson led a varied life. He tried farming for some time before setting up as a shipbuilder in the 1890s. From 1896 to 1904 Watson's Fore River Ship and Engine Company at Quincy, Massachusetts, built a range of vessels including battleships and schooners. In 1904 he switched careers once more, and trained for three years at the Massachusetts Institute of Technology as a geologist. He spent some time unsuccessfully searching California and Alaska for something of value to mine.

Watson finally became an actor at the age of 54 and took on roles in plays by William Shakespeare (1564–1616) at Stratford-on-Avon, England. In 1912 he returned to his home in Braintree, Massachusetts. He spent the rest of his life in amateur dramatics, writing his autobiography, *Exploring Life* (1926), and giving interviews about his time with Bell.

place of tuning forks in their device. One of the reeds had stopped vibrating and Watson gave it a tap. In a distant room Bell heard a loud twang—sound had been transmitted. On February 14, 1876, Bell filed a telephone patent application at the United States Patent Office, giving him the right to be the only person to make and sell his invention for a limited time. Just a few hours later, another patent for a telephone was filed from a rival, Elisha Gray (1835–1901). This would lead to the first of many challenges to Bell's patent (see box on page 72). However, on March 7, the Patent Office issued the patent to Bell for "the method of, and apparatus for, transmitting vocal or other sound telegraphically by causing electrical undulations...."

Bell's notebook entry of March 10, 1876, describes the exciting events of the day, as Watson took his place in one room with the "Receiving Instrument," and Bell took up position in another room next to the "Transmitting Instrument." Bell shouted into the transmitter, "Mr. Watson—Come here—I want to see you," and his notebook records what happened next. "To my delight he came and declared that he had heard and understood what I said. We then changed places.... The sentence, 'Mr. Bell do you understand what I say? Do—you— un—der—stand—what—I—say?' came quite clearly...." The new invention stole the show at the 1876 Centennial Exhibition in Philadelphia. Emperor Pedro of Brazil (1825–1891) is said to have dropped the machine in alarm, crying, "It talks!"

EXPERIMENTS WITH LIGHT

Bell continued to work on other methods of communication. His next project was the "photophone," or light-sounder. In the early 1870s it had been discovered

Thomas Watson is seen here with a model of Bell's first telephone.

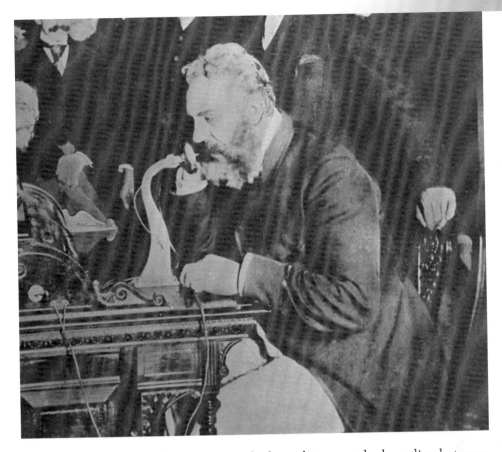

Here Alexander Graham Bell inaugurates the long-distance telephone line between New York and Chicago in 1892.

that the electrical resistance of the element selenium varied with the intensity of the light falling on it. Bell thought he could see in this a way to use a beam of light to transmit speech. A speaker's voice made a beam of light vibrate. The vibrating light beam was directed onto a piece of selenium, altering its resistance and thereby producing a varying electric current that could be turned back into sound.

Bell became very excited by this idea and he achieved some initial success in developing it. In 1880 he and his assistant, Charles Sumner Tainter, managed to transmit a photophone message from one building to another. "I have heard a ray of the sun laugh and cough and sing. I have been able to hear a shadow," Bell said. His enthusiasm was not shared by investors, though, who were more interested in putting money into the new telephone system.

This photo shows an early model of Bell's tetrahedral kite. A later model 40 feet across was able to carry a person through the air.

TO THE SKIES AND SEAS

Bell's natural curiosity had already led him onto a range of other projects. In 1901 he invented the tetrahedral kite—a kite with four triangular sides. This proved to be a very successful design, and he experimented with building gigantic versions, capable of carrying people. With four colleagues, and funding from his wife Mabel, in 1907 he formed the Aerial Experiment Association (AEA). On February 23, 1909, the AEA's biplane, the Silver Dart, was the first heavier-than-air craft to fly in Canada.

Bell also spent much time and money trying to develop a reliable and efficient hydrofoil craft. A hydrofoil is a boat that has "wings" placed under the hull that are connected to the boat by vertical spars. When the boat accelerates the wings develop "lift" and help raise the hull out of the water. This reduces drag on the hull and so allows the boat to travel much faster than a normal craft.

In 1906 Bell began work on his "heavier-than-water" machine. His first model, the HD-1, had encouraging results in tests, reaching a speed of 50 mph (80.4 kmh) before breaking up. Bell continued to work on and off on the project for the best part of a decade. When the United States entered World War I in 1917 Bell tried to interest the Navy in his new model, HD-4. Trials went well, and the hydrofoil reached a top speed of 54 mph (87 kmh). Although the Navy thought that the craft was too fragile for active service, the HD-4 set a world marine speed record that would not be broken until 1963.

SEEKING ANSWERS UNTIL THE END

A more personal quest was Bell's attempt to develop a "vacuum jacket." His baby son, Edward, had died in 1881 of breathing problems, and Bell wanted to design

The Silver Dart was made of steel, bamboo, wire, wood, and friction tape. The wings were covered with silver balloon cloth, a type of strong cotton fabric.

PROFESSOR BELL IN LYCEUM HALL, SALEM, ADDRESSING A PARTY OF SCIENTIFIC MEN IN BOSTON.
ACHUSETTS,—TRIAL EXHIBITION OF BELL'S TELEPHONE FOR THE TRANSMISSION OF SOUND BY ELECTRICITY, OPERATED BETWEEN SALEM AND B
MARCH 15TH.—FROM SKETCHES BY E. R. MORSE.—SEE PAGE 61.

Bell, seen here demonstrating the telephone, continued to experiment in his later years in areas such as magnetic fields and alternative fuels.

a jacket that would help people breathe by reducing the air pressure around the body. Once that had been done, atmospheric pressure forced air through the patient's mouth and into the lungs. Although this type of device would later—as the "iron lung"—be widely used to help patients with the infectious viral disease polio, it attracted little interest at the time.

Bell died on August 2, 1922, busy to the end. As he had told a reporter a few months earlier, he had continued trying to "seek answers for his unceasing hows and whys about things."

SCIENTIFIC BACKGROUND

Before 1870

Danish physicist Hans Christian Oersted (1777–1851) shows that an electric current produces a magnetic field

English physicist Michael Faraday (1791–1867) induces electric current by disrupting a magnetic field

American inventor Samuel Morse (1791–1872) patents the telegraph

1870

1875

1875 In Boston, Massachusetts, Bell and his assistant Thomas A. Watson (1854–1934) transmit sound electronically for the first time

1876 Bell sends the first long-distance telephone message 8 miles (13km) from Paris, Ontario, to Brantford, Ontario

1880

1880 In his laboratories at Baddeck Bay, Nova Scotia, Bell sends the first wireless telephone message by "photophone" (lightphone)

1881 Bell designs the vacuum jacket, a forerunner of the iron lung

1886 Bell sets up the Volta Bureau in Washington, D.C., for research to help the deaf

1885

1890

1890

1891 The American scientist and engineer Samuel Langley (1834–1906) begins work with Bell on problems of flight

1895

1896 Italian physicist Guglielmo Marconi (1874–1937) obtains a patent to use electromagnetic waves "for the purpose of wireless telegraphy"

1900

1901 Marconi makes the first transatlantic radio transmission from Cornwall, southwest England, to St. John's, Newfoundland, Canada

1903 At Kitty Hawk, South Carolina, brothers Orville (1871–1948) and Wilbur Wright (1867–1912) fly the first piloted airplane

1905

1906 At Baddock Bay Bell begins work on hydrofoil speed boats

1909 French aviator Louis Blériot (1872–1936) flies from Baraques, France, to Dover, England

1910

After 1910

1915 The first transcontinental telephone line links New York and San Francisco

1956 The first transatlantic telephone cables are laid

1962 Telstar is the first communications satellite to be launched

POLITICAL AND CULTURAL BACKGROUND

1869 In Montana the Union Pacific and Central Pacific Railroads make a transcontinental link

1873 New York's first streetcar goes into operation

1876 General George Custer (1839–1876) leads 264 men of the U.S. 7th Cavalry to their death at the hands of Sioux warriors in "Custer's Last Stand," on the Little Bighorn river in Montana

1883 American showman William Frederick "Buffalo Bill" Cody (1846–1917) begins a tour of the United States and Europe with his Wild West Show

1884 In Barcelona, Spain, work begins on the ornate and fantastical Sagrada Familia church, designed by Antonio Gaudí (1852–1926); it is still under construction today

1890 At Wounded Knee Creek, South Dakota, the U.S. 7th Cavalry massacre 200 Sioux men, women, and children

1895 In Germany, Rudolf Diesel (1858–1913) invents the diesel engine

1898 In the Spanish-American War, the United States acquires Puerto Rico, Guam, and the Philippines, and Cuba wins its independence from Spain

1903 The first baseball World Series takes place in the United States

1911 In China the Kuomintang "Revolutionary Alliance," under the leadership of Sun Yat-Sen (1867–1925) depose the last ruler of the Qing dynasty, the child emperor Pu Yi (1906–1967), and form a republic

acoustics The science of sound or the sound qualities of, for example, a room, theater, or concert hall.

amplifier A device that increases the strength of a sound or of an electronic signal representing a sound, as in a radio or hi-fi.

amplitude The intensity of a wave. The amplitude of a sound wave is directly related to its loudness.

analog Describing a signal or display that continuously varies. An analog signal resembles what it represents: For example, the groove on a traditional vinyl record is like a picture of the changing amplitude of the sound. See also *digital*.

antinode A position in a standing wave at which the amplitude is greatest. See also *node*.

anvil Also called incus, a small anvil-shaped bone in the middle ear that helps transmit sound from the eardrum to the inner ear.

auditory canal The passage that runs from the visible ear, or pinna, into the head.

bel (B) A unit of loudness named after the Scottish-born American inventor Alexander Graham Bell. In practice, the decibel is used instead.

CD Abbreviation for compact disc, a medium for recording sound, images, and data. It consists of a metal-coated plastic platter on which digital information is recorded as a track consisting of tiny pits.

cochlea A spiral organ in the inner ear that contains fluid and has many nerves attached. It is responsible for the detection of sounds.

deafness Complete or partial inability to hear.

decibel (dB) A unit of loudness equal to one tenth of a bel. If a sound is 10 dB louder than another one, it is 10 times as intense; if it is 20 dB louder, it is $10 \times 10 = 100$ times as intense, and so on.

density The mass of a substance per unit volume.

digital Describing a signal or display that uses digits (numerals) to represent something. For example, the display on a digital watch represents time as numbers rather than by the movement of hands. See also *analog*.

Doppler effect The change in frequency of a wave caused by the relative motion of the source and the observer. For example, the pitch of an ambulance siren seems to fall as the vehicle passes, then recedes from a listener.

ear The organ of hearing. In human beings it is a complex structure consisting of the outer ear, middle ear, and inner ear.

eardrum Also called tympanum, a membrane separating the outer ear from the middle ear. It vibrates when sound waves strike it, passing the vibrations to a chain of small linked bones in the middle ear.

echo A sound that is reflected from some surface or object before reaching a listener and so is delayed in relation to the main sound, which arrives directly.

echolocation Finding the direction and distance of an object by beaming sound pulses at it and detecting the echoes. The technology used is called sonar.

energy The capacity to do work. Sound waves can do work, so they contain energy. Energy must be used up to generate sound.

force An influence that changes the shape, position, or movement of an object.

frequency For a sound wave the number of times per second that the air molecules (or the molecules of whatever material the wave is traveling through) vibrate.

fundamental The lowest frequency in a sound that consists of a mixture of tones of different pure frequencies.

hammer Also called malleus, a small bone in the middle ear that helps transmit sound from the eardrum to the inner ear.

harmonic A frequency that accompanies the fundamental frequency in a sound and is in a simple numerical relation to it (e.g., 2, 3/2, or 5/3 times the frequency).

infrasound Sound of frequency too low to be heard by human beings.

inner ear The part of the ear that contains the organs of hearing and balance. See also *cochlea; semicircular canals.*

intensity In relation to sound the physical strength of a sound wave. The faster and farther that air molecules vibrate in a sound wave, the more intense the sound is.

labyrinth A complex structure in the inner ear consisting of the cochlea, the semi-circular canals, and the vestibule, to which the semicircular canals are joined.

larynx Also called the voicebox, the organ in the human throat that contains the vocal cords.

longitudinal wave A wave in which the vibrations are in the direction in which the wave itself moves. Sound waves are longitudinal. See also *transverse wave.*

loudspeaker A device that produces sound from an electrical signal.

Mach number The ratio of the speed of an object to the speed of sound.

magnetic tape A plastic tape coated with a magnetic material that can record sounds and other forms of information. The strength of magnetization of the tape at each point represents the loud-ness of the sound at a particular moment.

microphone A device that detects sounds and converts them into electrical signals that can be recorded or transmitted over wires or as radio or TV waves.

middle ear The section of the ear in which sound vibrations are transmitted from the eardrum to the organs of hearing in the inner ear.

node A position in a standing wave at which the amplitude is zero (or smallest). See also *antinode.*

noise A sound, especially one that is unde-sired because it is loud, unpleasant, or out of place.

octave 1. The interval in pitch between two notes, one of which has twice the fre-quency of the other. 2. A sequence of eight consecutive notes beginning and ending on two such notes.

outer ear The visible ear, or pinna, and the auditory canal, which leads from it.

pinna The visible flap of the ear, on the out-side of the head.

pitch The perceived "highness" or "lowness" of a sound. It depends on which frequen-cies are strongest in the sound.

power The rate at which energy changes. A definite amount of power is used in mak-ing a sound.

pressure The amount of force pressing on a particular area. Pressure is high in a wave of high intensity or loudness.

P wave Abbreviation for primary wave, a longitudinal seismic wave (from an earthquake) that acts in the direction of the disturbance causing the earthquake. See also *S wave.*

resonance Any vibration, or increase in vibration, that is caused by something else vibrating nearby. For example, when a musical note is sounded near a piano, strings in the piano tuned to the same pitch, or to a harmonious pitch, will vibrate because of resonance.

seismometer A device that measures the strength of the shock waves from seis-mic tremors (earthquakes). Similar devices are called seismographs.

semicircular canals Loop-shaped, fluid-filled organs in the inner ear that provide the sense of balance.

shock wave A disturbance that moves through a fluid, such as air or water, faster than the speed of sound in that fluid. See also *supersonic flow*.

sonar See *echolocation*.

standing wave A wave motion that does not move overall. There is vibration at stationary nodes, separated by antinodes where there is little or no vibration. It occurs in, for example, a plucked string on a musical instrument, where a wave traveling in one direction is reflected back from one fixed end. The two waves traveling in opposite directions combine to make a standing wave.

stationary wave Another name for a standing wave.

stirrup Also called stapes, a small stirrup-shaped bone in the middle ear that helps transmit sound from the eardrum to the inner ear.

subsonic flow Flow of a fluid at less than the speed of sound in that fluid. It is smoother and more regular than supersonic flow.

supersonic flow Flow of a fluid at more than the speed of sound in that fluid. It is marked by shock waves. See also *subsonic flow*.

S wave Abbreviation for secondary wave, a transverse seismic wave (from an earthquake) that is perpendicular to the direction of the disturbance causing the earthquake. S waves travel through the solid layers of the Earth, but not the liquid core. See also *P wave*.

timbre The distinctive quality of a sound. It is timbre that distinguishes different musical instruments that are sounding notes of the same pitch.

tone A musical sound, especially if it has a well-defined pitch, or the timbre of a musical sound.

transverse wave A wave in which the vibrations take place at right angles to the direction in which the wave itself moves. The vibrations of a plucked string, for example, are transverse, but sound waves are longitudinal waves.

traveling wave A moving pattern of disturbance in a material caused by the vibration of the material's particles, which do not move overall. See also *stationary wave*.

tympanum See *eardrum*.

ultrasound Sound of frequency too high to be heard by human beings.

vocal cords The elastic organs in the throat that produce the human voice by vibrating as air is expelled between them.

voiceprint A graphical representation of the intensity of each frequency of sound present in a sample of a person's speech. It can identify the person and sometimes reveal their emotional state.

wave A regularly repeating movement in the particles of a substance. Although there is no overall movement of the particles, the pattern of disturbance may move, forming a traveling wave, or may be fixed, forming a stationary wave.

wavelength The distance between two successive locations where a wave is at its maximum intensity.

Alexander Graham Bell National
    Historic Site of Canada
P. O. Box 159
Baddeck, Nova Scotia
Canada
B0E 1B0
902-295-2069
Web site: http://www.pc.gc.ca/lhn-nhs/
    ns/grahambell/index.aspx
Located near Alexander Graham Bell's
    summer home, this 25-acre prop-
    erty is home to the Alexander
    Graham Bell Museum, which fea-
    tures artifacts such as Bell's library
    and a full-scale replica of the Silver
    Dart. Visitors can also make their
    own kite and discover more about
    the science of sound and silence
    that so interested Bell.

American Meteorological Society
45 Beacon Street
Boston, MA 02108
617-227-2425
Web site: http://www.ametsoc.org
This organization promotes research
    and sharing of information on the
    atmosphere and related sciences.
    The AMS publishes print and
    online journals and sponsors sev-
    eral conferences each year.

Helen Keller Birthplace, Ivy Green
300 North Commons Street, West
Tuscumbia, AL 35674
256-383-4066
Web site: http://www.helenkellerbirthplace
    .org/

At the age of 19 months old, Helen
    Keller developed at illness that left
    her blind and deaf. Alexander
    Graham Bell met Helen when she
    just six years old and connected
    her with a teacher named Anne
    Sullivan. Sullivan was able to work
    with Helen, who eventually learned
    to write and speak. Visitors to this
    museum can tour Keller's child-
    hood home and see many items,
    such as her collection of Braille
    books and Braille typewriter.

National Museum of Mathematics
11 East 26th Street
New York, NY 10010
212-542-0566
Web site: http://momath.org/
This museum, which opened in 2012,
    seeks to spark visitors' curiosity
    and illuminate the wonder of math-
    ematics in the world. Visitors can
    experience hands-on exhibits, such
    as Math Midway, and take advan-
    tage of a lecture series called Math
    Encounters.

National Music Museum
The University of South Dakota
414 East Clark Street
Vermillion, SD 57069
605-677-5306
Web site: http://orgs.usd.edu/nmm/
    index.html
This museum, located at the University
    of South Dakota, houses over
    15,000 American, European, and non-

Western musical instruments from many cultures and historical periods. The museum also presents concerts, seminars, and conventions.

Rhythm! Discovery Center
110 W. Washington Street, Suite A
Indianapolis, IN 46204
317-275-9030
Web site: http://rhythmdiscoverycenter
.org/
The museum explores the role of rhythm and percussion in the shaping communication, music, art, performance, and society. Visitors can feel the vibrations of sound as they strike an 8-foot gong and hear the different pitches and timbres of a log drum. Other exhibits explore the history of the drum set and introduce percussion instruments from around the world.

Smithsonian National Air and Space Museum
Independence Avenue at 6th Street SW
Washington, DC 20560
202-633-2214
Web site: http://airandspace.si.edu/
visit/mall/
This museum showcases the history of air and space exploration and features the Apollo 11 Command Module, the Albert Einstein Planetarium, an observatory open to the public, and much more.

WEB SITES

Due to the changing nature of Internet links, Rosen Publishing has developed an online list of Web sites related to the subject of this book. This site is updated regularly. Please use this link to access the list:

http://www.rosenlinks.com/CORE/Sound

Bacon, Tony. *History of the American Guitar, 1833 to the Present Day*. Milwaukee, WI: Backbeat Books, 2012.

Bader, Bonnie. *Who Was Alexander Graham Bell?*. New York: Grosset & Dunlap, 2014.

Baines, Anthony. *Woodwind Instruments and Their History*. Mineola, NY: Dover Publications, 2012.

Beranek, Leo L., and Tim Mellow. *Acoustics: Sounds Fields and Transducers*. Waltham, MA: Academic Press, 2013.

Berg, Richard E., and David G. Stork. *The Physics of Sound*. Boston: Addison-Wesley, 2004.

Cox, Trevor. *The Sound Book: The Science of the Sonic Wonders of the World*. New York: W. W. Norton & Company, 2014.

Dean, Matt. *The Drum: A History*. Lanham, MD: Scarecrow Press, 2012.

Denny, Mark. *Blip, Ping, and Buzz: Making Sense of Radar and Sonar*. Baltimore, MD: Johns Hopkins University Press, 2008.

DK Publishing. *Music: The Definitive Visual History*. New York: DK Publishing, 2014.

Dolge, Alfred. *Pianos and Their Makers: A Comprehensive History of the Development of the Piano*. Mineola, NY: Dover Publications, 2012.

Grant, R. G. *Flight: The Complete History*. New York: DK Publishing, 2007.

Gray, Charlotte. *Reluctant Genius: Alexander Graham Bell and the Passion for Invention*. New York: Arcade Publishing, 2011.

Keller, Helen. *The Story of My Life*. New York: Signet Classics, 2010.

Nicholls, Jeff. *The Drum Book: A History of the Rock Drum Kit*. Milwaukee, WI: Backbeat Books, 2009.

Phelps, Mark. *Flight: 100 Greatest Aircraft*. San Francisco: Weldon Owen, 2014.

Simon, Seymour. *Earthquakes*. New York: HarperCollins, 2006.

Taylor, Timothy D., Mark Katz, and Tony Grajeda. *Music, Sound, and Technology in America: A Documentary History of Early Phonograph, Cinema, and Radio*. Durham, NC: Duke University Press Books, 2012.

Wade-Matthews, Max. *The Encyclopedia of Music: Musical Instruments and the Art of Music-Making*. London: Anness Publishing, 2012.

PHOTO CREDITS